FOLK NEW YEAR PICTURES

FOLK NEW YEAR PICTURES

Compiled by Lan Xianlin

 FOREIGN LANGUAGES PRESS

First Edition 2008

ISBN 978-7-119-04675-4

©Foreign Languages Press, Beijing, China, 2008

Published by

Foreign Languages Press

24 Baiwanzhuang Road, Beijing 100037, China

http: //www. flp. com. cn

Distributed by

China International Book Trading Corporation

35 Chegongzhuang Xilu, Beijing 100044, China

P.O. Box 399, Beijing, China

Printed in the People's Republic of China

Contents

INTRODUCTION

New Year Picture (*Nianhua*) derives its name from the age-old custom of Chinese New Year decorations. A fascinating and popular art form, it in fact constitutes a separate branch of traditional Chinese painting. The concept of New Year Picture refers to painted works made by local workshops and regularly posted inside and outside homes. New Year Picture encompasses all such paintings reflecting rural and urban lives, handmade by folk artisans, as well as those carved or produced and painted in local workshops. Chinese New Year Picture possesses colorful detail with abundant cultural and historical connotations.

Origins

As an old genre of painting, inspired and improved by ancient ceremonial customs, Chinese New Year Picture originated around the 11th century BC, when deities related to nature were the most important subjects. In ancient times, people felt deep reverence toward these deities, and monarchs would make sacrificial offerings each year to the "Five Sacred Mountains" (Mount Tai, the Sacred Eastern Mountain in Shandong; Mount Hua, the Sacred Western Mountain in Shaanxi; Mount Heng, the Sacred Southern Mountain in Hunan; Mount Heng, the Sacred Northern Mountain in Shanxi; and Mount Song, the Sacred Central Mountain in Henan) and the "Four Sacred Rivers" (the Yangtze, Huaihe, Yellow, and Jishui rivers

Illustrations of *Women's Ethical Code*: a famous painting made in the Song Dynasty (960-1279) according to the classic *Women's Ethical Code*, authored by Madam Zheng of the Tang Dynasty (618-907), intended to cultivate female conduct under feudal China. This is a picture to illustrate the content of the book; Song Dynasty (960-1279), Anonymous

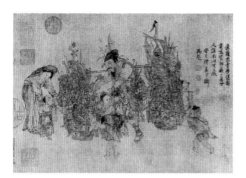

Itinerant Peddler:
Southern Song Dynasty, Li Song

The scroll of Lotus and Mandarin Ducks:
Southern Song Dynasty (1127-1279), Li Song

– considered to represent the River God for the Chinese nation). Meanwhile, ceremonial offerings to local deities, town deities, mountain deities and the Dragon King were likewise conducted among the people each year.

The Door God and Kitchen God played major roles during the time of the Shang and Zhou dynasties (1600-256 BC). Artistic images of the Door God and Kitchen God were handed down from the Han Dynasty (206 BC-220 AD). Historical records of that time mentioned two Door Gods named Shen Tu and Yu Lei (brothers experienced in catching ghosts: if any demons dared plague people, they would catch and bind them as food for tigers; later on, people painted the two brothers' images along with tigers on their doors to ward off evil). The images of four deities, Qinglong (Green Dragon), Baihu (White Tiger), Zhuque (Vermillion Bird) and Xuanwu (Black Warrior), were regarded as auspicious symbols during the Han

Illustrations from local operas,
Ming Dynasty (1368-1644)

Beauties: Sui Dynasty,
Linfen, Shanxi Province

4

Dynasty (206 BC-220 AD). In those days, New Year Pictures were painted directly onto doors, gradually fading away over the years. Although no longer seen today, we can still imagine how splendid these had been, through the tomb frescoes, portrait stones and bricks preserved from those times.

The Tang Dynasty (618-907) was one of the most powerful feudal empires. Skills in folk paintings became greatly inspired, thanks to vast economic advancement and cultural prosperity. The subject matter of paintings was broadened extensively. It was said that Zhong Kui (a Chinese folklore deity who drives away evil spirits) could catch and eat evil ghosts while escorting the Son of Heaven (the emperor). So his image was favored among the people during this time. With the emergence of pictures of maids or beauties, subjects reflecting common lives began to enter the social scene.

The Song Dynasty (960-1279) was a period of growth. A prosperous economy, advanced technology in handicraft, and emphasis on culture offered requisite nourishment for the growth of New Year Pictures. "Paper pictures" expanded extensively into mass quantities through the development of printing craft, accompanying the emergence of numerous professional workshops. New Year Picture was successfully transformed from being only religious iconography into a daily commodity, and gradually became a popular folk art form. It began to depict everyday life and reflected agricultural production and daily living. Subject matters, such as household Door Gods in the form of civil officials, beauties, cute babies and other new themes, gradually emerged. Ultimately, New Year Pictures became indispensable decorations for the Chinese New Year.

The Ming Dynasty (1368-1644) was a period of maturity. Book illustrations became popular at that time. Printing technology exceeded all previous dynasties. Furthermore, the craft of carving became more accomplished, while chromatography skills achieved continuous innovation. The technology of woodcut printing to a large extent drove the prosperity of New Year Pictures. Two woodcut printing centers were established. Beijing acted as the center in the north, while the southern center encompassed Nanjing, Suzhou, Hangzhou and Jianou. Under the influence of the two centers, groups of New Year Picture production bases, including Yangliuqing in Tianjin,

Zhong Kui on an Inspection Tour: mid-13th century, Gong Kai

One-Hundred Fortunes: Ming Dynasty

5

Yangjiabu in Shandong, Zhuxianzhen in Henan and Taohuawu in Suzhou, emerged one after the other. New Year Picture themes in the Ming Dynasty added new elements built on the essentials passed down from previous dynasties. For instance, Qin Qiong, a famous general of the Tang Dynasty (618-907) and Yuchi Gong (another famous Tang general) became new idols for military Door Gods.

New Year Picture attained its peak during the Qing Dynasty (1616-1911) in three successive stages. The recovery stage spanned from 1662 to 1736, due to the stability of regime and the development of social production. New Year Picture referring to farming and weaving, cute babies and other subjects reflecting filial piety, righteousness and civilization prevailed at this time. By building on traditional arts, it attained even higher quality in the period 1736-1796 due to the development of the economy and the prosperity of society. New Year Picture picked up a great deal from local operas, novels and other related genres, as well as absorbing essential skills and expressive styles from European prints. The most important subjects at that time in New Year Pictures belonged to historical stories, legends and mythologies, local operas, as well as landscapes and scenic spots. With domestic crises and foreign invasions after 1821, the whole nation suffered a huge blow and started to wane. By that time, themes, influenced by the current politics, began to criticize the ills of the times and reflect the call for social reform.

Ten Kings of the Palace of Hell
(Yama, one of ten kings in the
Palace of Hell in Chinese folklore):
Ming Dynasty

Pavilions in the Western Regions:
Qing Dynasty, Beijing

Wang Zhaojun Marrying a Tibetan Chieftain (the picture shows the beautiful Wang Zhaojun marrying a Tibetan Chieftain for the country in 36 BC): Qing Dynasty, from the collection of Li Cunsong

During the period of the Republic of China (1912-1949), New Year Pictures not only described traditional folk lives but also reflected the new fashions and morality of the society. Thus, it was also referred to as "New New Year Picture." For instance, calendar pictures became a favorite vehicle. With the rise of lithographic printing, a type of calendar printed with new lunar dates emerged in Shanghai, and was often given as gifts when lottery tickets were sold, and the calendar was named *Hujing Kaicai Tu* (*The Opening Ceremony of Lottery Issue in Shanghai*). Scenic sites in Shanghai, flowers, characters and sales materials for the lottery were all imprinted. It harmoniously combined forms of traditional Chinese New Year Picture with manifestations of Western paintings, with vivid colors and smooth depictions of scenery. There was also another genre of New Year Picture in the form of vertical scroll, which were used for advertising such items as cigarettes.

Introduction

Types and Styles

Numerous varieties and different appellations for Chinese New Year Pictures made classification extremely complicated.

1. Classification by Technology

Print Blocks This variety takes the lead in all types, with both monochromic prints and color paintings. Core technologies are woodcut and prints.

Hand-drawn The oldest New Year Pictures were drawn manually. These included "*Pu Hui*", outlined with the carbon and ash from burned willow branches, only produced in Gaomi, Shandong Province; and "*Feng*", which took the phoenix as its subject, made in Fengyang, Anhui Province. During the process of making "*Pu Hui*", artisans would put the rough sketch, drawn with carbon and ash, on formal rubbing paper and complete the whole picture on it, featuring bold lines and smooth dyes.

Half-printed and Half-drawn This variety is a combination of printing and drawing. Artisans usually cut wood to make a block model first, and then print ink lines and part of the background colors on it. The following are steps in the sketching of contours and the painting of colors. New Year Pictures made in Yangliuqing, Tianjin and Mianzhu, Sichuan, all belong to this variety.

Military Door Gods: Sichuan Province

Door Gods, lintel pictures and
door couplets: Qi'ao, Zhuhai

11. Classification by Usage

Door Pictures Pictures posted or directly drawn on doors were called door pictures. Door pictures possess a long history and can be dated back to the Shang and Zhou dynasties (1600-256 BC). People posted these types of pictures on doors not only for warding off evil spirits, but also as decoration.

Center Piece in a home:
Shi Family Compound, Tianjin

Paper-cuts at civilian residences
in northern China: Wuqiang, Hebei

Gods of Earth and Heaven:
Zhima, Baoding, Hebei

Zhizha (paper handicrafts used for
ceremonial offerings): Dongshi, Hubei

Lintel Pictures This variety was mostly made in rectangles, with three or five of them posted on the lintel of the door to attract good fortune. Lintel pictures were used as decorations for festive occasions, and at weddings and funerals. In some regions, they were hung above beds or shrines. They were usually cut and engraved with red paper, with some of them using multicolor paper. Auspicious symbols epitomized these pictures.

Door Couplets These long and narrow door couplets were always hung in pairs. The contents include auspicious calligraphy or the composition of characters and paintings named "*Huaniaozi*" (flower-and-bird paintings with inscriptions).

Barn Pictures These pictures were usually posted on the fencing of barns, including pictures of a "*Lanmenpan*" (deity guarding livestock), "*Niuyin*" (posted by barns to protect livestock), etc. *Lanmenpan* usually had such images as the Judge of the Hell or Zhong Kui (a deity who drives away evil spirits). It was also called "*Dazhugui*," which means, "to ward off evil spirits that harm livestock." According to folk custom, people posted these pictures on the railings of pens to protect pigs from the plague. *Niuyin* could also be posted on railings of barns with images of the Ox King, the Horse King and pictures of Dozens of Piglets, etc.

Centre Piece Centre Piece, with a panoramic design, could be unfolded vertically downward from the top, and was usually hung in the sitting-room. People liked to mount them as scroll pictures, adding a couple of couplets on either side. It involved broad and extensive themes with auspicious purposes.

Window Pictures This variety contained diverse themes, including written characters, human figures, animals and flowers.

Paper-cuts for Window Decoration Paper-cuts are also called small-scale New Year Pictures and mostly painted with colors.

Kangweihua This was a type of New Year Pictures posted at the head of a *kang*. The *kang*, a heated brick bed with two walls opposite each other and the third adjoining side with a window, is a major resting site for residents in northern China. So, *kangweihua* are posted on three adjoining walls, stressing the panorama of the pictures and including a series of themes.

Xiangdishu A bride's parents would have secretly hidden *xiangdishu* at the bottom of a chest as part of their daughter's dowry. Their content resembled formal New Year Pictures, but containing some erotic images that were used to impart sex education to the daughter.

Zhima *Zhima* (paper printed with images of idols and burned as ceremonial offerings) were used for burning during folk rituals. People usually chose rough and single-color materials to make *zhima* and made them in a rather slapdash fashion.

Lantern Pictures Auspicious pictures, symbols, stories of local operas are the chief content in Lantern Pictures (a type of New Year Pictures used to decorate colorful lanterns). A lantern usually has four pictures on it. They have gripping plots and vivid images, and very often connected to each other in content.

III. Classification by Regional Features

Yangliuqing New Year Pictures of Tianjin Yangliuqing New Year Pictures were named after the town of Yangliuqing in Tianjin. Initiated between 1628 to 1644, the town's New Year Pictures production became famous for over 300 years. It reached a peak during the first half of the 18th century to the second half of the 19th century. More than 20,000,000 pieces were made and printed annually from the late 19th century to the early 20th century. The most exquisite were presented to the court as tribute. Local peasants were engaged in making New Year Pictures throughout most of the year; each family became good at dyeing and clever at painting. Although Yangliuqing New Year Pictures are considered folk handicraft, they indeed possess much potential as high art. Deeply influenced by Chinese traditional painting skills and not only picking up technologies of wood engraving from the art academies of the Qing Dynasty (1644-1911) but also from a European perspective, they gradually developed an exquisite and elegant style appealing to the tastes of all kinds of people, with well-rounded drawings and vivid and harmonious colors. Yangliuqing New Year Pictures cover a wide variety of subject matter, including Door Gods, cute babies and beauties, folklore, mythology, local opera characters, mountains and waters, birds and flowers, and anything one could wish for.

Expressing sincere gratitude to the benefactor: memorial tablet, Fujian

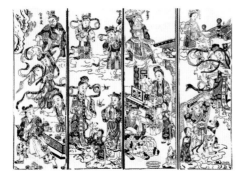

The Cowherd and the Weaver Girl,
legendary lovers from ancient China:
Wuqiang, Hebei

Pictures of figures, mountains and rivers:
Wuqiang, Hebei

Wuqiang New Year Pictures of Hebei Wuqiang New Year Pictures originated in the early 15th century. They had long been produced in large quantities in Wuqiang, which enjoyed the reputation of being the "Hometown of Chinese New Year Pictures." The engraving skills for plate making mainly depended on relief carving, supplemented by intaglio carving. The whole work would appear dynamic, bold and well spaced. With well-organized composition, clear themes and clear-cut images, Wuqiang New Year Pictures were quite appropriate for decoration, full of strong rural flavor. The subject matter involved stories and local operas, as well as everyday life, cute babies and beauties, mountains and rivers, birds and flowers, etc.

Zhuxianzhen New Year Pictures of Henan Zhuxianzhen New Year Pictures can be dated back to the Song Dynasty (960-1279). Artisans adopted the handicraft of watercolor block printing on a wood plate and followed the engraved-printing technologies of the Song Dynasty. The carvers' skills were simple and succinct. Colors stressed the contrasts of yellow and purple, with strong visual effects. The pictures possessed bold and vigorous strokes, well-rounded composition, vivid colors and exaggerated models. The unsophisticated styles of the Central Plains' cultures, which had deeply influenced the neighboring regions, were completely embodied in the content of the subject matter, as well as in the manufacture and methods of their handicraft. The subject matter covered three principal categories,

Wealthy with Vast Riches, as Lucky as You Wish: Weifang, Shandong

including the exorcism of evil spirits, along with blessings, customs and traditions, as well as stories and local operas.

Weifang New Year Pictures of Shandong Weifang, the kite capital, is also famous throughout the country for its New Year Picture block-prints. The most well known, with a long history of more than 300 years, were made in Yangjiabu. Hundreds of New Year Picture workshops were found all over the town at the end of 19th century. In early times, artisans here adopted half-printed and half-drawn skills to make New Year Pictures, influenced by the styles of Yangliuqing pictures. Later on,

Returning Home after Making a Fortune:
Fengxiang, Shaanxi

Three Wise Old Men Watching
a Chess Game: Fengxiang, Shaanxi

Art master, Zhang Dianying carving
in a New Year Picture workshop:
Weifang, Shandong

Printing handicrafts, Qingyunshan
New Year Picture Workshop:
Weifang, Shandong

Craft of dyeing and painting:
Yangliuqing New Year Picture
Workshop , Tianjin

they compared and gathered experience from Taohuawu pictures of Suzhou, and eventually formed their own unique style. Nowadays, New Year Pictures made in Weifang possess both the robustness of the northern schools and the delicateness of the southern schools, alongside distinctive local features. The mainstream method of Weifang New Year Pictures is block printing, which possesses vivid models and regular lines, in addition to stressing primary colors. It covers extensive subjects, including daily life, auspicious pictures, drama stories and folklore, etc.

Jinnan New Year Pictures Linfen and the surrounding areas in Shanxi Province are the centers of Jinnan New Year Pictures. Linfen, called "Pingyang" in ancient times, was a block-printing center through the 12th and 13th centuries. The jute paper for painting and calligraphy abundantly produced here provided excellent material and technological support. There are two different handicrafts for making Jinnan New Year Pictures: the first one involves skilled work using a natural style to be printed on an ink line plate and then painted manually; the other one, with a plain, bold and vivid style, involves complete color printing in black, yellow, scarlet, pink and green.

Painting craft: Fengxiang Yinian New Year Picture Workshop, Shaanxi

Fengxiang New Year Pictures of Shaanxi Originating in the 7th century, and peaking through the 14th to the 19th centuries, Fengxiang New Year Pictures possessed a natural but flamboyant style with a long history. It usually adopted manual printing technology with manual dyeing in part, and pursued a strong color contrast through manual smudging of dyes in certain spaces, highlighting contours by golden or argent colors. Exaggerated models maintained a simple art form and possessed strong local features.

Taohuawu New Year Pictures of Suzhou Taohuawu New Year Pictures originated in the Ming Dynasty (1368-1644). They had long been popular across Southeast Asia and greatly influenced Japanese Yamato-e. Simultaneously influenced by illustrations of traditional engravings and European etchings in early times, Taohuawu New Year Pictures stressed perspective drawing and an exquisite style in the early days. The later color technology of relief carving was well composed with flawless drawings and carvings. As dominant colors, vivid yet elegant pink and pinkish green embodied the strong folk flavor of areas south of the lower reaches of the Yangtze River. The subjects refer to folk deities, cute babies and beauties, daily life, sceneries of mountains and rivers, flowers and fruits, etc.

Mianzhu New Year Pictures of Sichuan Mianzhu New Year Pictures have made Mianzhu famous, a city well known in China for its bamboo paper. Besides adjoining Chengdu, which is famous for engraving works, Mianzhu offered advanced technology and material conditions for the development of New Year Pictures. It was said that more than 300 New Year Picture workshops emerged in its heyday. The techniques of Mianzhu New Year Pictures may be divided into two different varieties. The first one belongs to colored drawing, and the second to block-print rubbings. The former stresses techniques of both carving and drawing, with features of vivid colors and unaffected creations. Artisans usually carve the ink lines first, then trace them with ink, and paint the colors last. They cover a great variety of subjects, the most distinctive including Door Gods, cute babies and beauties as well as folklore. The latter specialized in woodcut and ink prints. With a sensible and simple style, its subject matter include images of folk deities, folklore, master calligraphy as well as paintings, and pictures of cultivation and weaving, etc. In the past, artisans living in Mianzhu usually used surplus materials to make some private works for extra earnings. Unrestrained works with bold but concise styles, vigorous images and fluid drawings, such as painted door pictures, usually sold at night fairs, were the most characteristic of Mianzhu.

Twelve Flower Gods (cards made of wood plates through carving and painting): Taohuawu, Suzhou

Goddess Delivering a Baby: Fengxiang, Shaanxi

18

Fujian New Year Pictures Fujian New Year Pictures had, to some extent, gained from its association with engraved literary works, which had existed in Fujian from the 14th to 17th centuries. Quanzhou, Zhangzhou and its environs were principle production centers. With a strong local flavor in handicrafts with simple but powerful styles, Quanzhou New Year Pictures usually selected red paper as the background printed with black lines, and colors of yellow, green, white and blue. Door pictures and other auspicious patterns, like "Bringing Money and Treasure", were the favorite subjects. Zhangzhou door pictures mostly favor red paper and using pinkish green, pinkish yellow, pinkish blue and other colors for printing. The main subjects consisted of customs, current affairs, local operas and stories. Door pictures posted on temple gates sometimes selected black paper as background, with colors of pinkish blue, vermilion and other hues for printing. The main subjects consisted of some composite pictures and each of them comprised four separate sectors, for instance, four deities named Fu, Lu, Shou and Xi (respectively happiness, remuneration, longevity and good luck); four beasts – the elephant, lion, tiger and leopard; and four seasonal flowers – the peony, lotus, chrysanthemum and Chinese plum flower. Generally, New Year Pictures selected white paper as background with color compositions of ink lines in red, orange, green and other colors.

DOOR GODS

Door Gods

As a unique subject and principal genre for New Year Pictures, the Door God is a deity that can ward off evil spirits and guard a house. Door Gods come in two varieties: one is the civil Door God and the other is the military Door God. The tiger and the rooster have also been taken as Door Gods for a long time.

Military Door Gods

Military Door Gods consist of a symmetrical duo, and are usually posted on the two boards of the main door or an inside door for warding off evil spirits and guarding the house.

Ling Bao Shen Pan: Fengxiang, Shaanxi

Ling Bao Shen Pan

Deities with the ability to drive away evil spirits were called "Pan Guan" (the Judge) in Chinese folk engravings. Ling Bao Shen Pan, also known as Zhong Kui in Chinese folklore, could drive away demons and eat them, to guarantee the safety of the house. In the pictures, he usually looks awe-inspiring, holds a sword, wears a red robe and exhibits a horrible glare.

Ling Bao Shen Pan: Fengxiang, Shaanxi

Shen Tu and Yu Lei

As the earliest Door Gods, Shen Tu and Yu Lei were powerful deities in Chinese folklore who specialized in fighting demons. Legend tells us that Shen Tu and Yu Lei were brothers adept at catching ghosts. If any evil infested and plagued people, they would catch and bind them up to feed tigers. Later, people used to paint on doors the brothers' images along with tigers, to ward off evil spirits. This custom has passed down to this day.

Shen Tu and Yu Lei: Weifang, Shandong

Shen Tu and Yu Lei: Fengxiang, Shaanxi

Qin Qiong and Jingde

They have been the most popular Door Gods from the Ming and Qing dynasties (1368-1911) onwards. It was said that Emperor Taizong of the Tang Dynasty had suffered a complicated disease that gave him nightmares. In his dream, he was often harassed by ghosts throwing stones or tiles outside his palace. After hearing of this situation, the generals Qin Qiong and Jinde volunteered to guard the emperor on three consecutive nights. It actually worked and the emperor's malady was exorcised. Taking the fatigue of the two meritorious generals into account, the emperor ordered court painters to post two generals' images on doors, instead of having them personally present. So, common people also followed the lead of their emperor and regarded the two generals as Door Gods, a custom which was handed down from generation to generation. On New Year's Eve, Chinese people post the two generals' images on doors to ward off evil spirits and guard the whole family.

Qin Qiong and Jingde: Liaocheng, Shandong

恭賀佳節

Qin Qiong and Jingde: Fengxiang, Shaanxi

秦琼坐虎

陕西凤翔北小里工美组

General Qin Qiong Standing on a Tiger Skin:
Fengxiang, Shaanxi

General Jingde Standing on a Tiger Skin:
Fengxiang, Shaanxi

敬德坐虎

北小里王義組

28

Randeng Taoist Priest and Zhao Gongming

The two characters both come out of the ancient Chinese mythological novel *Feng Shen Yan Yi (Canonization of the Gods)*. They fought loyally for their masters and were usually considered equal in strength. Thus, people became used to regarding these Door Gods as a pair. Legend recalled that the four Military Gods of Fortune, named Zhaocai, Zhaobao, Nazhen and Lishi, led by Zhao Gongming, were put in charge of bestowing happiness and blessings, and pursuing escaped criminals. In the picture, Zhao Gongming rides a black tiger, weaves an iron whip, and uses, as his magic weapons, a pair of gold dragon scissors in addition to a pearl that pacifies the rolling waves; the Taoist Priest rides a spotted deer and uses a Heaven-and-Earth ruler.

Zhao Gongming: Zhuxianzhen, Henan

Randeng Taoist Priest: Zhuxianzhen, Henan

Horse-riding Door God: Fengxiang, Shaanxi

Guan Gong and Guan Sheng: Wuqiang, Hebei

Guan Gong and Guan Sheng

Guan Gong was a famous general in the period of the Three Kingdoms (220-280). Guan Sheng was a hero from *Outlaws of the Marsh*. The two different heroes were joined because of their same surname "Guan" and both used a broadsword as a weapon. Thus, they are also known among the people as "Broadsword Door Gods."

Zhao Yun

Zhao Yun, born in Shu (present-day Sichuan Province and surrounding areas), was known as a valiant general of Liu Bei (founder of the Kingdom of Shu, AD 221-263). Zhao Yun had long been regarded as a folk idol due to his loyalty to the Kingdom of Shu. The symmetrical left and right door pictures show an image of Zhao Yun riding a horse in armor, embracing his master's son who he had saved, and holding his spear. His image as a Door God is very popular in Shandong, Henan and surrounding areas.

Zhao Yun: Liaocheng, Shandong

Erect Hammer Door God: Mianzhu, Sichuan

Erect Hammer Door God: Mianzhu, Sichuan

Dear-riding Door God: Jinnan

Tiger-riding Door God: Jinnan

Broadsword Door Gods: Tantou, Hunan

Door Gods

Five Sons Door God

The Five Sons Door God originated from a story describing a tale of five sons passing the imperial civil examinations. It was said that Dou Yujun, who lived in Five Dynasties (907-960), was extremely strict with his five sons and regularly volunteered to establish free schools and employ famous scholars for impoverished students. His five sons, named Yi, Yan, Kan, Cheng and Xi consecutively, passed the imperial civil examinations. The typical scene of the five sons' story showed five children holding flowers and wares and clustering round a civil official. Another famous picture, named *Wu Zi Duo Kui* (*Five Children Compete to be Chief*), showed one child holding a cap and the other four clustering round him and scrambling for the cap. The Chinese character "魁" means the "highest grade" and sounds like another Chinese character "盔," which means "helmet." So, the child who holds the helmet in the picture symbolizes achieving success and coming out first in the highest imperial examination. Liangping New Year Picture of Five Sons Door Gods, which signifies teaching children, guarding the house and hoping for prosperity for the family, shows a picture of five children clustering round a military general.

Five Sons Door God: Liangping, Chongqing

Twin Genii He-He Door God: Liangping, Chongqing

Twin Genii He-He Door God

According to legend, two close deities named Hanshan and Shide fell in love with the same woman at the same time. However, they were unaware of this coincidence until Hanshan was preparing to marry her. After he understood what had happened, he resolved to shave his head and become a monk. Shide also left her and became a monk, to accompany his friend. They established Hanshan Temple. In the past, people used to hang their images in the central room on their wedding day, because the twin genii He-He were considered deities of happiness. The two deities were usually pictured as two children, with one of them holding a lotus and the other holding a round box. Sometimes, five bats were pictured as flying out of the box, which symbolized harmony and a well-matched couple. The image of the valiant general in the picture gave people a feeling of security. People posted this type of Door God in the form of a general or twin genii He-He (He means harmony and being together), hoping to ward off evil spirits and to bring blessings on the whole family for a harmonious life.

Broadsword Door God: Mianzhu, Sichuan

Iron Staff Wielding God: Mianzhu, Sichuan

Iron Staff Wielding God

The Iron Staff Wielding God is a unique form of Door God picture only produced in Mianzhu, Sichuan. Two famous generals of the Tang Dynasty (618-907) Qin Qiong and Jingde are pictured as Iron Staff Wielding Gods looking dynamic and neat, with strong local features.

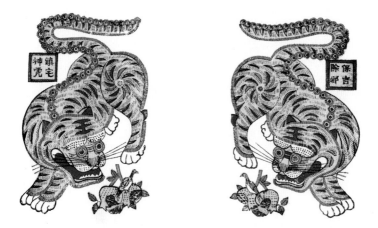

Tiger Spirit Guarding the House: Weifang, Shandong

Tiger Spirit Guarding the House

Known as a king of beasts, the tiger was regarded as an auspicious animal by people. The custom of taking the tiger as a Door God has existed for a long time. Legend tells us that the tiger could eat evil ghosts, ward off demons and bless families.

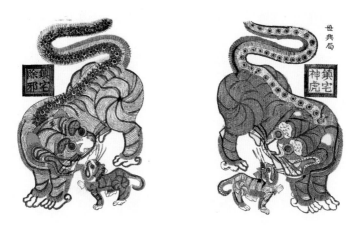

Tiger Spirit Guarding the House: Fengxiang, Shaanxi

Civil Door Gods

Civil Door God pictures are usually posted on the inside doors of the yard, with the hope of seeking blessings and happiness. They are usually classified into two varieties: a symmetrical pair for a door with two boards, and a single one for one-board door.

God of Prosperous Country, Happy People and Favorable Weather

This is considered a Civil Door God. A benign civil official in court dress and hat with an official tablet (usually held before the chest by officials when received by the emperor), followed by a child who holds a streamer on which "Prosperous Country, Happy People and Favorable Weather" are written, is pictured with the hope of being blessed by the heavens.

God of Prosperous Country, Happy People and Favorable Weather: Fengxiang, Shaanxi

Civil and Military Door Gods

This type of Door God picture consists of a refined civil official with a white face, and a valiant military general with a black face. The civil and military Door Gods embodied people's wishes for all-round blessings. A military general was seen as being able to ward off evil spirits and guard the house, while a civil official was to bless the whole family.

Civil and Military Door Gods: Fengxiang, Shaanxi

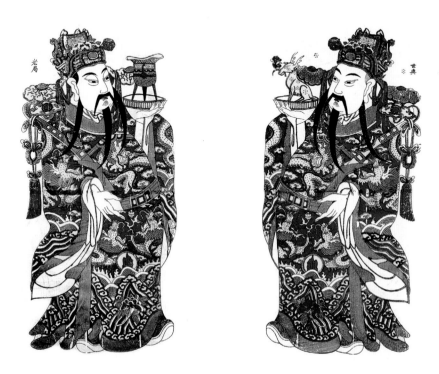

Promoting Official Rank and Increasing Wealth: Fengxiang, Shaanxi

Promoting Official Rank and Increasing Wealth

The two mirror-image civil officials shown in the picture hold an official tablet and a salver in their right and left hand, respectively. There are flowers, *jue* (ancient three-legged wine vessel with a loop handle), coronets, deer and other items placed on the salver. The flower signifies passing imperial examinations successfully; *jue* means achieving a title of nobility; the coronet implies official rank, and the deer is symbolic of "wealth." A high wealth always goes with high official rank, so wealth advancement and official rank promotion became a type of universal pursuit in feudal society.

Number One Scholar Holding a Gold Ingot

The one who came out first in the highest imperial examination was called "Number One Scholar" in the past. So, the title of Number One Scholar became the first goal for scholars, because the Number One Scholar would be conferred official rank by the emperor and enjoy a luxurious life. The picture shows a Number One Scholar holding a gold ingot, embodying people's prevalent pursuits.

Number One Scholar Holding a Flower: Mianzhu, Sichuan

狀元進寶

狀元進寶

Number One Scholar Holding a Gold Ingot: Fengxiang, Shaanxi

Eternal Spring in the World

It was also known as "*Liu He Tong Chun*." Liu He means the "whole world," and *Tong Chun* means eternal spring. So *Liu He Tong Chun* means eternal spring all over the world. In Chinese, "鹿" (*lu*, deer) is pronounced as "六" (*liu*, six) in southern China and "鹤" (*he*, crane) is homophone of "合" (*he*, harmony). The deer and crane in China symbolize "longevity." Usually, *Liu He Tong Chun* consists of two varieties of pictures. One is a composition of a deer, crane, flowers, pines, Chinese toons, etc.; while the other is of a deer, crane and an official. This picture belongs to the latter, embodying hopes for official rank, promotion and longevity in life.

Eternal Spring in the World: Mianzhu, Sichuan

Eternal Spring in the World: Mianzhu, Sichuan

Five Sons Door God (signifying educating children, guarding the house,
and blessings from the heavens): Jinnan

FOLK DEITIES

Folk Deities

Numerous folk deities have long been enshrined among the people in China. The most conspicuous feature of Chinese folk custom is the worship of numerous deities, including the natural deities of the sun, moon, mountains and rivers, and the daily deities of clothing, food, household and customs in China's history. These deities were also enshrined through Buddhism, Daoism and Confucianism.

Enshrined Deity Images

Images of deities worshipped all year round were mostly made with colorful print blocks.

Goddess of Mercy: Wuqiang, Hebei

Guanyin

Guanyin (Goddess of Mercy) is a Mahayana Bodhisattva. She could embody 32 types of incarnations to liberate all human beings and often practiced on Mount Putuo in the East China Sea. Guanyin has long been considered a graceful and compassionate-faced goddess in people's hearts, because she was always infinitely merciful, saving people in difficulties.

Guanyin: Yangliuqing, Tianjin

Eight Immortals

According to ancient Chinese mythology, the Eight Immortals were Han Zhongli, who always holds his magic fan; Zhang Guolao, who carries his fisherman folk drum; Han Xiangzi, who melodiously blows his flute; Li Tieguai, who has a gourd tied to his waist; Cao Guojiu, who holds a jade tablet; Lü Dongbin, who always carries a sword; Lan Caihe, who carries a flower basket; and, He Xiangu, the only female immortal among them, who carries a lotus flower. They eventually became immortal after long years of austere religious cultivation and delivered people from suffering. The Eight Immortals are still revered to this day among the people.

Lü Dongbin and Li Tieguai:
Weifang, Shandong

Han Zhongli and Cao Guojiu:
Weifang, Shandong

Zhang Guolao and Han Xiangzi:
Weifang, Shandong

Lan Caihe and He Xiangu:
Weifang, Shandong

Zhong Kui

It is said that Zhong Kui was a palace graduate during the Wude Period (AD 618-627) of the Tang Dynasty (618-907). He had gone to the capital for the final imperial examination and was dismissed due to his ugly appearance. He became so enraged that he wildly hit his head fatally on a side-step. After he died, he arrived in hell and killed several evil spirits. The Jade Emperor of Heaven conferred the title Master of Exorcising Evil Spirits on him for his contribution. Another legend recounted that, during the Kaiyuan Period (713-742) of the Tang Dynasty, Emperor Xuanzong had several times seen Zhong Kui catching a demon in his dreams, so he ordered painters to draw Zhong Kui's image and hang it in the palace to ward off evil spirits. Thus, the custom of hanging Zhong Kui's image in houses has been passed down to this day.

Zhong Kui:
Zhuxianzheng, Henan

Zhong Kui Killing Ghosts: Weifang

Heavenly Master Zhang Daoling Killing Evil Spirits:
Fengxiang, Shaanxi

Heavenly Master Zhang
Daoling: Jinnan

Heavenly Master Zhang Daoling

Zhang Daoling was the founder of Daoism, and
had the power to exorcise evil spirits, according to
legend. He is revered by the people as divine. He
is pictured riding a fierce tiger, with a sword in his
hand and brandishing his magic weapon to drive
away evil spirits and animals.

Three Gods

These three deities in Chinese legend were in charge of happiness, wealth and longevity. The God of Happiness in court dress, with a *ruyi* (an S-shaped wand) in his hand, distributes disaster and happiness; the God of Wealth in official uniform, with a fan in his hand, distributes poverty and wealth; and the God of Longevity, an old man with a white beard, distributes life and death. People worship these three deities for blessings on their families, and for wealth and longevity.

The God of Longevity:
Wuqiang, Hebei

Three Gods:
Yangliuqing, Tianjin

The God of Happiness: Weifang, Shandong

The God of Happiness

People usually post the image of the God of Happiness on their doors, with the hope of bringing blessings on their whole family during the Chinese New Year.

God of Wealth

People usually worship two different Gods of Wealth – the military God of Wealth and the civil God of Wealth. The two famous courtiers, Bi Gan (1092-1029 BC) and Fan Li (517 BC-?), were highly regarded and worshipped as civil Gods of Wealth. The two valiant generals, Guan Yu (160-219) and Zhao Gongming (a character in Chinese folklore), were worshipped as military Gods of Wealth. These illustrious personages lived in different times. Bi Gan, executed by his king, was a loyal courtier and was worshipped by the people as a civil God of Wealth. Fan Li became a hermit and successful merchant, after he assisted his king to fulfill great deeds. Guan Yu, a famous general, was worshipped as the God of Wealth among the people due to his loyalty. Zhao Gongming, who took charge of wealth, in folklore could prevent complicated diseases and ward off disaster.

神　財

定福宮

God of Wealth: Fengxiang, Shaanxi

God of the Hearth

The God of the Hearth was worshipped widely among the people and regarded as a house deity who could bless all family members. Thus, Chinese people became used to presenting ceremonial offerings to this God of the Hearth. On every 24th day of the 12th lunar month, each family would post images of the God of the Hearth, make melon-shaped cakes and burn joss sticks to make ceremonial offerings to him, to bring good fortune for the whole family. New Year prints of the God of the Hearth possess different varieties and styles in the different regions of China.

God of the Hearth: Weifang, Shandong

God of the Hearth: Fengxiang, Shaanxi

God of the Hearth and His wife:
Fengxiang, Shaanxi

Storehouse God

Chinese people believed that a storehouse was the most important place to deposit property and that it must be guarded by deities. The Storehouse God is pictured in a red robe with a black gauze cap on his head. Two young attendants stand to his right and left. The partition board behind him is decorated with designs of vases and fruit bowls, and the couplet written on it expresses hope that infinite wealth would never be wasted due to the protection of the Storehouse God.

Storehouse God: Fengxiang, Shaanxi

Local God of the Land: Weifang, Shandong

Local God of the Land

The Local God of the Land was widely worshipped among people in China. People thought that all cities, villages, residences, temples, hills and mountains were protected by different Local Gods of the Land, and each person born there would be protected by them. Although the Local Gods of the Land possessed a lower rank, they were responsible for the resources of those lands, which were significant in people's lives. People usually sought help from them when they were confronted with danger. Widely worshipped, only two- to three-feet high shrines of the Local Gods of the Land covered all villages throughout China. Images of the Local God of the Land were posted on family shrines.

Local God of the Land: Fengxiang, Shaanxi

Horse King and Cattle King

Horses and cattle are very closely related to people's daily lives and production. In the past, peasants and horse owners would buy images of the Horse King and the Cattle King and post them on byres and stables before the Chinese New Year. The Horse King was pictured to the left, as a general in armor with three eyes and four arms. The Cattle King was pictured to the right, as a civilian official in court dress, with a white face and black beard.

Horse King and Cattle King: Fengxiang, Shaanxi

Dragon King: Fengxiang, Shaanxi   Bimawen: Fengxiang, Shaanxi

Dragon King

In the past, people classified dragons into four varieties: the first one was called the Heavenly Dragon, and guarding the heavens; the second was the Magic Dragon, controlling the rain; the third was the Earth Dragon, who controlled springs and water resources; and the fourth was Treasure-keeping Dragon, guarding all treasures under the heavens. However, the two Dragon Kings worshipped among the folk were the Magic Dragon (in charge of water and drought) and the Earth Dragon (in charge of harvests and famines). People would go to the Temple of the Dragon King to make ceremonial offerings, hoping for abundant rain when drought endangered harvests.

Bimawen

Bimawen was a folk deity who could keep horses immune from plagues, and his image was usually posted in stables. In the Chinese classic novel *Journey to the West*, the Jade Emperor of Heaven conferred the title "Bimawen" to the Monkey King. So people changed, according to Chinese homophony (for *bimawen*), "庇马翁" (a herder of horses) into "弼马翁" (a deity who can make horses immune from plagues), with the hope of passing on blessings to horses.

Gods of Heaven and Earth

Chinese people liked to assemble all deities on one page, including the deities of Confucianism, Buddhism and Daoism, alongside the folk deities. Different pictures of Gods of Heaven and Earth acquired variations in different places, but would be more or less designed layer upon layer horizontally, followed by the names, and reflect the concept of worship of multiple deities among the people. They were posted and enshrined in central halls during the Chinese New Year in the past, or burned in rituals as *zhima* (paper printed with images of idols, to be burned as ceremonial offerings).

Gods of Heaven and Earth: Baoding, Hebei

Long Feng Qian Ma (designs of dragons, phoenixes, coins and horses, for bringing fortune and good luck): Fengxiang, Shaanxi

Mighty Gods from the Ten Directions in the Universe: Fengxiang, Shaanxi

Gods from the Ten Directions in the Universe: Wuqiang, Hebei

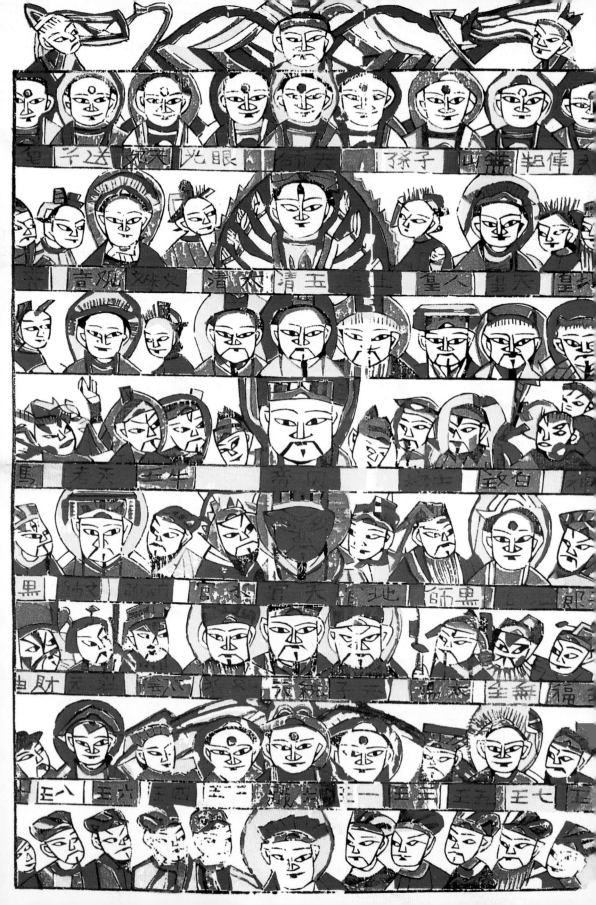

Ceremonial Deity Images

People usually burnt images of deities to worship the heavens after ceremonial offerings. These images were printed in single colors, and usually resembling *zhima* (prints of idols, burned as ceremonial offerings).

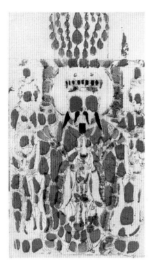

God of Mount Tai:
Yuhang, Zhejiang

Guanyin: Jingzhou, Hubei

Sacred Eastern Mountain

The Sacred Eastern Mountain was also called the God of Mount Tai. The sacrificial ceremony for the Sacred Eastern Mountain was initiated by Qin Shi Huang (246-209 BC), the first Emperor of the Qin Dynasty (221-207 BC), and continued to be practiced by later emperors, who conferred on it the title of Great Emperor of the Sacred Eastern Mountain. Gradually, the authority and function of the God of Mount Tai changed to take charge of life and death. So, people would prepare fruit and other offerings to revere the Great Emperor of the Sacred Eastern Mountain at every ceremonial offering, such as driving away evil spirits, leading one's soul to the heavens, extending a dying person's life by borrowing a life span from a relative, releasing souls from purgatory, and hunting and driving away demons, etc.

◀ Gods of Heaven and Earth: Wuqiang, Hebei

Seven Goddesses: Fujian

Envoy of Incantations

Incantations were figures and charms used in magic and sorcery, aimed at averting calamity and treating diseases. The Envoy of Incantations was a unique type of *zhima* (paper printed with images of idols, burned as ceremonial offerings) produced in Fujian and surrounding areas. The Envoy of Incantations, in court dress with an official hat on his head like a civil courtier, is pictured as holding incantations and riding on a galloping horse. This design was meant to inspire the Envoy of Incantations to send incantations in a hurry, so as to guarantee the safety of the country or the home.

Envoy of Incantations: Fujian

Mazu: Fujian

Mazu

Mazu, a legendary goddess mainly for the coastal areas of southeastern China, was a sea deity worshipped by fishermen. According to legend, Mazu was exceedingly clever from childhood, and adept at celestial knowledge and medical science. Furthermore, she was also able to predict the weather for fishermen, as well as shelter them. Thus, people loved, worshipped and regarded her as a sea deity, due to her public-spirited and righteous behavior. Mazu Temples are widespread in the provinces of Fujian, Taiwan and Guangdong.

De Zhai Fang Chun: Fujian

A Tiger Holding a Sword in the Mouth: Fujian

De Zhai Fang Chun

Used as a family memorial tablet, a type of *zhima*, produced in Fujian and surrounding areas as a ceremonial offering to ancestors, *De Zhai Fang Chun* was usually pictured as a family ancestral hall with male and female ancestral images on top, ancestral tablets in the middle, a hall gate at the bottom, and family members standing on the two sides. An inscribed board with the four eye-catching Chinese characters, meaning "house filled with spring," written on it was hung in memorial halls, with hopes for enduring prosperity and happiness for the entire family, with high morality and infinite mercy.

A Tiger Holding a Sword in the Mouth

People usually posted this picture on door heads, for warding off evil spirits and blessing the whole family.

Gods of Fortune from Five Directions

One popular conception prevailing among the people was that the wish for bringing in fortune could be realized by burning ceremonial offerings to the deities of the roads. In the past, merchants would make ceremonial offerings to the five Gods of Fortune of the East, South, West, North and Central, before reopening their businesses on the fifth day of each Chinese New Year.

Gods of Fortune from Five Directions: Shanxi

Three Gods: Fujian

Local God of the Land: Shanxi

CUTE BABIES AND
BEAUTIES

Cute Babies and Beauties

They have been major themes in folk New Year Pictures, as a way of praying to the heavens for granting a baby and prosperity for the whole family. People have long favored these types of beautiful images with auspicious wishes.

Cute Babies

Being most abundant in the content of New Year Pictures, images of cute babies were used to express good wishes at every festive occasion.

Happiness, Wealth and Having Many Children (composite picture consisting of a bat, crane, guava and a child): Yangliuqing, Tianjin

Bearing Sons One after Another: Yangliuqing, Tianjin

Bearing Sons One after Another

This is a composite picture consisting of a lotus flower, sweet-scented osmanthus, *sheng* (reed pipe wind instrument), carp and a baby, signifying the bearing of many babies with good destinies. In China, "lotus flower, sweet-scented osmanthus, *sheng*, carp and baby" would be chanted continuously, in hopes of bearing many babies with good destinies. The lotus and carp possess numerous seeds and eggs, so this composite picture symbolizes bearing numerous offspring and prosperity for the whole family.

Living a Rich Life Year after Year:
Yangliuqing, Tianjin

First Place in the Second-class Imperial
Examination: Yangliuqing, Tianjin

Living Rich Life Year after Year

The pronunciation (*lian*) of the Chinese character for lotus "莲" is quite similar to the character "连," meaning "consecutive"; as are the characters for fish "鱼" and surplus "余" (*yu*). So, this composite picture consists of a child, carp, lotus, etc., signifying a happy and rich life year after year.

Abundant and Comfortable Life Year after Year

In this composite picture, a cute baby rides on a carp's back while holding a sweet-scented osmanthus flower next to a blooming peony, which signifies a happy and rich life year after year. As mentioned above, the characters for "fish" and "surplus" are pronounced similarly in Chinese, as are the characters for osmanthus "桂" and wealth "贵" (*gui*).

First Place in the Second-class Imperial Examination

The picture showed reeds and two crabs. The top class in the imperial civil examination system was called the palace examination which had three levels. The first three places in the first-class palace examination were respectively called *Zhuangyuan*, *Bangyan* and *Tanhua*. The first place in the second-class palace examination was called *Chuanlu*. Names of those who passed the palace examination usually were put at the bottom of the list, which was made of straw paper. The two crabs stood for the second-class palace examination, and the Chinese words "芦" (*lu*, reeds) and "胪" (*lu*) are pronounced similarly. So, the composite picture was designed to mean passing the palace examination and achieving the first four places.

Spring Ox

The ox was the prime animal power for farming and symbolized wealth and spring. According to old custom, peasants would hold a special ceremony on the first seasonal division point (the 4th or 5th day of the 2nd lunar month) called "*bianchun*," which meant "whipping" to begin the spring cultivation. At the ceremony, peasants would dress up like "*Jumangshen*" (God of the Spring, in charge of spring farming) and whip an ox, usually made of earth or paper, to invoke blessings on people and animals at the beginning of spring. The whole ceremony was usually called "*bianchun*."

Abundant and Comfortable Life Year after Year: Yangliuqing, Tianjin

Spring Ox: Yangliuqing, Tianjin

Winning Laurels in the Moon Palace

Two children are pictured playing with each other in the Moon Palace. One plays with gold coins, while the other teases a toad with sweet-scented osmanthus. There were also longan ("dragon eye") fruit, which meant coming first in the imperial civil examinations, first in the provincial capital, then the national capital and finally the palace, as well as a "bow" and "bat" signifying happiness, and the peony symbolizing nobility. Acquiring sweet-scented osmanthus from the Moon Palace meant passing imperial civil examinations and achieving high rank.

Winning Laurels in the Moon Palace: Yangliuqing, Tianjin

福到我家

Happiness Coming into the House: Yangliuqing, Tianjin

Ten Trades

This was a type of balladeering accompanied by a gong, drums, cymbals and other percussions. The performer sitting behind the shelf would beat a *danpi* drum (small drum-like instrument for coordinating the other musical instruments in Chinese opera) and a big drum hit with a hammer using one hand, while using the other hand to beat the gong by pulling a string. His feet had to step on a pedal connected with the big cymbal, while he had to sing continuously. As a unique performance produced in Yangliuqing, Ten Trades was very popular during the Qianlong Period of the Qing Dynasty (1736-1796).

Ten Trades: Yangliuqing, Tianjin

Cute Babies and Beauties

Ten Trades: Yangliuqing, Tianjin

Auspicious Qilin Delivering a Baby

This showed a qilin (or kylin) coming into the house with a baby on its back on auspicious clouds. According to folk belief, the qilin was an animal of benevolence, which could bring sons to people. It was said that if you sincerely worshipped the qilin, you would be guaranteed a son. Besides, people usually call virtuous and genial descendants with literary talents "son of qilin."

Auspicious Qilin Delivering a Baby: Wuqiang, Hebei

Great Luck on Lunar New Year's Day: Wuqiang, Hebei

Lucky Stars Bringing Fame and Fortune

As the harbinger of dawn, the rooster was regarded as the deity of brightness, and an auspicious fowl that could ward off evil spirits with civil, military, brave, benevolent and honest virtues. The Chinese character "鸡" is pronounced "*ji*" like "吉," so the crowing of roosters symbolize "fame and fortune." Two children are pictured in embroidered coats with crowns on their heads sitting on a rooster's back, and holding banners with characters meaning good luck, high official and wealth. Bats symbolizing happiness are also pictured as flying around the children, to signify great luck and a bright future.

Genial Temper Making Fortunes

Also known by another name, *Harmonious Whole*, this picture was first created by Emperor Zhu Jianshen (1447-1488) of the Ming Dynasty (1368-1644), who very much favored painting. He put three famous persons: Huiyuan, Lu Jingxiu and Tao Yuanming, all from the Jin Dynasty (265-420), together in one picture. His particular design had three persons sitting in a circle and embracing each other, with their faces appearing as the same one from front and side views. Simultaneously, there is a cute baby sitting in the circle when viewed as a whole. But if you scan it carefully, you will also make out three persons sitting in a circle. This unique design symbolized a harmonious combination of Buddhism, Taoism and Confucianism. The child in the picture is all smiles and holding a scroll with characters signifying harmony, happiness and good luck on Lunar New Year's Day.

Genial Temper Making Fortunes: Tantou, Hunan

Heavenly Official Bestowing Happiness:
Weifang, Shandong

Heavenly Official Bestowing Happiness

The Heavenly Official, a deity who took charge of bestowing happiness, is the first of "Three Officials" of the Taoism, the other two being the Earth Official and Water Official. In folklore, the Earth Official provides reprieve from guilt, and the Water Official wards off adversity.

Hospitably Inviting the God of Happiness into the House: Weifang, Shandong

The Child Riding a Lion

A majestic-looking child is pictured as riding a lion with a flag in his right hand and a spear in his left. The awe-inspiring lion is the king of beasts, possessing high prestige and worshipped among the people for eliminating all harmful things and averting disaster.

Cute Child Playing the *Sanxian*

A cute child is pictured playing the *sanxian* (three-stringed plucked instrument). At the top of the picture are some captions: "Child sits at home, treasures rush through the door, *sanxian* melodies jingle, and all the five poisonous creatures (scorpion, snake, centipede, lizard and toad) are driven away from the house and the family is rich, noble and lucky. I act quickly as instructed by Taishanglaojun (supreme master of Taoism)." This auspicious picture was usually used to prevent children from being harmed by the five poisonous creatures.

Child Riding a Lion: Fengxiang, Shaanxi

Cute Child Playing the *Sanxian*: Fengxiang, Shaanxi

增 福 童 子

世興局

Child Bringing Happiness:
Fengxiang, Shaanxi

Cute Babies and Beauties

納祥童子

Child Bringing Luck:
Fengxiang, Shaanxi

Leading a Comfortable Life in Old Age:
Fengxiang, Shaanxi

Auspicious Happiness in Superabundance:
Fengxiang, Shaanxi

Leading a Comfortable Life in Old Age

A peony, butterfly and cat were pictured in this composite picture, so it also enjoyed another name, *"Mao Die Xiang Xi"* (*Cat and Butterfly Frolicking with Each Other*). This is because the Chinese character for cat "猫" is pronounced *"mao,"* like "耄" meaning "longevity;" as with the words for butterfly "蝶" and old age "耋", both pronounced *"die."* The peony also signifies "nobility" in China's folk tradition. Overall, this composite New Year print symbolizes nobility and longevity.

Auspicious Happiness in Superabundance

In this New Year print, a child holds a huge carp in his arms, carrying a long halberd on his back, with a stone *qing* behind him. The halberd is an ancient weapon, and the *qing*, an ancient percussion instrument. Successive pronunciation of the two words "戟" (*ji*, halberd) and "磬" (*qing*, the instrument) resembles "吉庆" (*ji qing*) in Chinese, as fish "鱼" and surplus "余" (*yu*) are likewise homophones. Thus, this composite New Year print consisting of these auspicious factors signifies harvest, wealth and a happy life.

Sweet Life in Four Seasons: Fengxiang, Shaanxi

Honors and Treasures Fill the House: Weifang, Shandong

Child Holding a Vase

A child holding a vase is pictured in this New Year print. The Chinese character "瓶" has a similar pronunciation (*ping*) to "平" meaning "peace." In the vase, these are usually the flowers of peony, lotus, chrysanthemum and Chinese rose, representing four seasons, and symbolizing safety all year round. A peony design on a vase signifies safety and nobility, while a lotus in a vase means safety over the coming years. It is usually put up on the door of a living room, as a way of seeing happiness whenever you enter the room, with the hope of guaranteeing the safety of the family and prosperity for descendants.

Children Holding Vases: Zhuxianzhen, Henan

Children with Treasure Vases: Mianzhu, Sichuan

Child Standing on a Lotus Flower: Mianzhu, Sichuan

Child Standing on a Lotus Flower

The child is pictured holding one lotus flower while standing on another. A lotus flower is also referred to as a "water lily." In Chinese, the character "莲" (water lily) has a similar pronunciation (*lian*) to "连" (consecutively), so this composite picture embodies the hope of bearing many babies consecutively as well as of prosperity for the family and an abundant proliferation of descendants.

Children with Treasure Vases

Two children are pictured holding treasure vases with cloud designs. The vase, inlaid with an ingot-shaped mountain, is held by the child on the right, while the child on the left holds a vase, with a "coin-bearing plant" in it. Furthermore, gold coins pour out of the two treasure vases, and bats fly around their feet. The gold coins symbolize treasure, and the bat stands for the advent of fortune. Thus, the picture invokes glory and wealth.

Children with Treasure Vases: Mianzhu, Sichuan

Ripe Pomegranate Containing Numerous Seeds

A couple of children are depicted pulling a boat loaded with dozens of pomegranates, while carrying a huge carp on their shoulders. The pomegranate and carp stand for the power of procreation, because a ripe pomegranate contains many seeds, while the carp contain many eggs. So, this composite picture has an auspicious meaning of prosperity for descendants.

Ripe Pomegranate Containing Numerous Seeds: Weifang, Shandong

Beauties

Subjects with beauties come in two varieties: those in ancient robes or those in fashionable dress. Beauties in ancient costumes usually belong to legends, while those in fashionable dress are women in real life.

Fairy Boy Delivering Treasures: Shandong

Fairy Boy Delivering Treasures

A woman in an embroidered dress holds a colorful banner with characters meaning "Fairy Boy Delivering Treasures" and a boy rides a crane with a glossy ganoderma in his hand. The crane is usually ridden by immortals and signifies "longevity;" the glossy ganoderma has function to save life from the brink of death, and to retain youth. The woman and the boy symbolize the prosperity of the family. Thus, this composite picture contains the meaning of prosperity for the whole family and longevity for descendants.

100

Abundant Happiness and Fortune

This picture shows us a young lady sitting cross-legged on a bed, accompanied by two children and a maiden holding a moon-shaped fan. One of the children is holding a halberd and the other is holding a citron. Two bats fly around them. "Bat" (蝠) is pronounced "*fu*" like "prosperity" (福); likewise "橼" (citron) and "缘" (good luck), "扇" (fan) and "善" (kindness), and "戟" (halberd) and "庆" (celebration) are all homonyms. So the overall meaning involves bringing fortune to the family through being ready to help others.

▶ Abundant Happiness and Fortune: Yangliuqing, Tianjin

A Boy Teasing a Frog

Two women nursing a boy, who teases a frog are pictured in this New Year print. The originator of human life was Nü Wa, who, according to legend, created human beings and patched the sky. The Chinese characters for "蛙" (frog) and "娃" (child) are homophonic, pronunced "*wa*", so the frog is regarded as a symbol of procreative love. As well, the frog was seen as beneficial to people and worshipped as a deity for its blessings and for warding off disaster. This New Year print contains the auspicious meanings of caring for children and maintaining the prosperity of the family.

A Boy Teasing a Frog: Yangliuqing, Tianjin

Mother and Son: Yangliuqing, Tianjin

Spring Outing of Beauties: Yangliuqing, Tianjin

Crab Feast at Ouxiangxie Pavilion: Yangliuqing, Tianjin

Crab Feast at Ouxiangxie Pavilion

Derived from an episode in the Chinese classic *A Dream of Red Mansions*, it tells how Shi Xiangyun hosted a crab feast at the *Ouxiangxie* Pavilion in the Grand View Garden and invited Mother Jia, Madam Wang, Sister Feng and other young women to enjoy the flower blossoms, taste the crabs, drink wine and compose poems.

Repeatedly Successful in Imperial Civil Examinations

This composite picture usually consists of a magpie, three litchis, three longan fruit and three walnuts. Furthermore, there is another variety also consisting of a child aiming a strung bow at three copper coins or shoe-shaped gold ingots. Thus, it was also called "*Lian Zhong San Yuan*" (repeated success in imperial civil examinations). This is because litchi, longan and walnut all have round fruit resembling balls, and the Chinese character "圆" (round) is pronounced "*yuan*", like "元" (first). During the Ming and Qing dynasties, the first candidate in any grade of the imperial civil examinations was called "元" (*yuan*). Those in the first place in a county imperial examination were called *jieyuan*, while first in the provincial examination were *huiyuan*, and top in the final palace examination were *zhuangyuan*. The one who could win consecutively in all imperial examinations was called "*Lian Zhong San Yuan*."

Good Tidings of Repeated Success in Imperial Civil Examinations:
Fengxiang, Shaanxi

尋倩
梅女

A Beauty Seeking a Plum Blossom:
Fengxiang, Shaanxi

Happy Harvest Returning of Fisherwomen

This picture shows a joyful scene of fisherwomen just returning from a fishing harvest. The fish is regarded as an auspicious creature among the people and filled with much emblematic meaning. The Chinese character "鱼" is pronounced "*yu*" like "余", which symbolizes surplus in life. Besides, the fish can bear numerous spawn, so it also symbolizes prosperity for the family and descendants. This New Year print signifies seeking superabundance and family prosperity in life.

Happy Harvest Return of Fisherwomen:
Fengxiang, Shaanxi

Surplus Wealth and Nobility:
Weifang, Shandong

Beauty Carrying an Umbrella on Her
Shoulder: Mianzhu, Sichuan

Two Beauties: Mianzhu, Sichuan

Beauty Holding an Umbrella in Hand:
Mianzhu, Sichuan

Beauties on a Spring Outing:
Mianzhu, Sichuan

CUSTOMS AND FESTIVALS

Customs and Festivals

As typical New Year Picture subjects that are closest to living reality, these images hold much significance, including daily life, auspicious symbols and wall calendars.

Daily Life

This type of New Year Pictures mainly reflect real life, including labor production, and social customs.

Welcoming the Bride:
Weifang, Shandong

Increasing Wealth over
Time, Blessings for Horses:
Weifang, Shandong

Fattened Pig Entering the House: Yangliuqing, Shandong

Fattened Pig Entering the House

As one of twelve symbolic animals and a treasure of peasant families, the pig is a token of good harvest and wealth. Chinese people regard the pig as auspicious livestock and have long worshipped it. A fattened pig, carrying a coin-bearing plant, treasure bowl or bulk grain container, entering your house during the New Year symbolizes good harvest and fortune.

Ten Labors of Men

The picture displays grand scenes of the labor of peasants during the spring and autumn, including plowing, seeding, weeding, harvesting, threshing, winnowing and packing. Corresponding to the "Ten Labors of Women", they reflect the division of labor among men and women in the farming society of ancient China.

Ten Labors of Men: Fengxiang, Shaanxi

Ten Labors of Men: Fengxiang, Shaanxi

Ten Labors of Women: Fengxiang, Shaanxi   Ten Labors of Women: Fengxiang, Shaanxi

Ten Labors of Women

The picture describes labor scenes of women in farming society, including fluffing cotton, spinning, making rope, pulling thread in weaving, weaving by loom, and cleaning. Women also needed to take care of children and feed livestock.

Treasure Bowl

A bowl, filled with gold coins, jewelry, gold ingots, coral and other valuable treasures, is pictured to signify flourishing business and great fortune. The treasure bowl originated in Chinese folklore. It was said that a poor man named Shen Wansan had seen hundreds of men in green clothes in a dream, who asked him for help. When day broke, he saw a fisherman about to kill hundreds of frogs, so Shen stopped him and bought all the frogs, to free them back into the pond. The frogs began croaking in the pond all night long. At dawn, Shen went to the pond to drive them away, but he saw the frogs holding up a bowl. Shen then took the bowl back home. The next day, while his wife was washing her hands in the bowl, she dropped her silver ring in it, and to her surprise, silver rings suddenly filled the bowl. They then put one gold ingot in the bowl, and likewise, a bowlful of gold ingots appeared. From then on, Shen Wansan became a rich man.

中国 朱仙镇木版年画社甲

A Harvest of 10,000 Taels of Gold: Zhuxianzhen, Henan

Treasure Bowl: Taohuawu, Suzhou

Spring Ox: Fengxiang, Shaanxi

Great Fortune: Zhuxianzhen, Henan

Definitely Becoming Rich This Year: Weifang, Shandong

Auspicious Pictures and Symbols

These types of New Year Pictures make full use of beautiful representations of reality, such as animals and flowers, to express good wishes.

Peony Blossom Representing Wealth and Fortune

As a unique flower originating in China, the peony is regarded as the king of flowers, with a ravishing beauty and heavenly fragrance. Peonies usually blossom with voluminous flowers and a strong fragrance in spring. Thus, they have a long history of being taken as a symbol of luck, nobility and prosperity. People like to use the peony as decoration to signify wealth and nobility.

Huge Vase: Wuqiang, Hebei

Peony Blossom Representing Wealth and Fortune: Taohuawu, Suzhou

Keeping Safe in the Four Seasons: Weifang, Shandong

Keeping Safe in the Four Seasons

The plum blossom, peony, lotus and chrysanthemum are all seasonal flowers that represent each of the seasons. It is also said that the asphodel, lotus, chrysanthemum and plum blossom are all seasonal flowers, too. Due to the homophony of vase "瓶" and peace "平" as "*ping*," this composite New Year print consists of seasonal flowers signifying safety all year round.

122

Happiness, Wealth, Longevity and Happiness:
Weifang, Shandong

Making What Is Good Still Better: Wuqiang, Hebei

Seasonal Birds and Flowers: Wuqiang, Hebei

Lion Playing with a Colored Silk Ball

As a king of the beasts, the lion is thought to ward off demons and guard houses. Moreover, the colored silk ball is also auspicious. Due to Chinese homophony, the lion and the colored silk ball represent official rank and power. In Chinese folklore, when a male lion teases a lioness and their body hairs entwine into a ball which will give birth to a baby lion. So, the lion playing with a colored silk ball also symbolizes descendants, procreation and family prosperity. People also transformed "The Lion Playing with a Colored Silk Ball" into the "Lion Dance," long popular among folk traditions to express happy and auspicious wishes.

Lion Playing with a Colored Silk Ball: Wuqiang, Hebei

Maintaining Love to a Ripe Old Age: Weifang, Shandong

Maintaining Love to a Ripe Old Age

This composite New Year print consists of a Chinese bulbul and peony, with a hidden meaning of maintaining love to ripe old age. The white-headed Chinese bulbul is usually used to represent elders. The peony stands for wealth and nobility. So, "Maintaining Love to a Ripe Old Age" is usually used for weddings.

Phoenix Paying Homage to the Sun

The phoenix is a legendary bird with a colorful head and wings. The phoenix is a king among birds and usually symbolizes talent. The sun shining its infinite brightness represents a sagacious ruler. So, this composite picture signifies talent appreciated by an enlightened ruler, and also contains a hidden meaning of talents emerging in the times of prosperity.

Phoenix Paying Homage to the Sun:
Weifang, Shandong

Boguwen (Designs Carved on Ancient Utensils)

The ethos of "back to the ancients" was popular in the time of the Northern Song Dynasty (960-1127). Emperor Huizhong (1101-1126) of the Northern Song Dynasty ordered his courtiers to collect and store all ancient utensils in the Xuan He Palace, compiling 30 volumes of *Collections of Utensils in Xuan He Palace*. So, later generations became accustomed to referring to designs carved on ancient utensils as "*Boguwen*." In auspicious design, "*Boguwen*" has become a symbol for opulent families and represents refined hermits with extensive wisdom.

Boguwen: Shizhuzhai, Suzhou

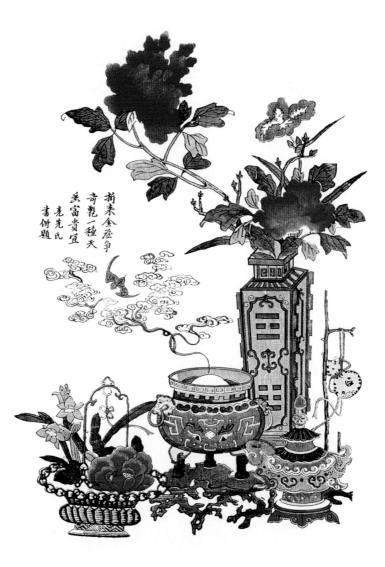

採来金蕊争
奇艳一種天
兵富贵宜
亮先氏
書仍題

Boguwen: Shizhuzhai, Suzhou

Fu Zi Shen Xian

This New Year print – popular in Suzhou and surrounding areas – was hung in the central hall. Actually, it is a huge Chinese character "福" (happiness) with illustrations in the contours of the strokes. Further, a blossoming peony served as a foil behind the character inlaid with many deity images, including the "God of Fortune Riding a Tiger," "Liuhai Teasing a Gold Toad," "Qilin Delivering a Baby," "Twin Genii He-He," "Number One Scholar," "God of Fortune Bestowing Happiness," and so on. This whole composite picture signifies blessing and nobility.

Couplet:
Wuqiang, Hebei

Fu Zi Shen Xian: Taohuawu, Suzhou

Couplet:
Wuqiang, Hebei

Hearth Gods: Zhuxianzhen, Henan

A page from calendar "24 Seasonal Division Points": Fengxiang, Shaanxi

New Year Calendar Print

As one form of New Year Pictures, the New Year calendar print made it very convenient for people to follow the annual calendar and its 24 seasonal division points, in order to arrange their farming lives accordingly. It was usually produced in mass quantities due to its enormous practicality and wide demand.

Introducing Division Points of the Next Three Years: Wuqiang, Hebei

Chasing away Cold for 81 Days: Wuqiang, Hebei

Chasing away Cold for 81 Days

This originated in the Song Dynasty. The weather gradually became colder and colder after the Winter Solstice, taking 81 days before peasants began their spring plowing in the Spring Solstice. Chasing Away Cold for 81 Days was used to count and reflect the changes in weather, with 81 plum blossom petals depicted, with one colored in each day to keep count. Different ways for marking different weather were adopted to precisely record the changes in weather, such as snowy, windy, sunny, cloudy, etc. It could help predict the situation of dry or wet soil and insect pestilence in the coming year.

STORIES AND DRAMAS

Stories and Dramas

As the most popular forms of New Year Pictures, originating in the Ming and Qing dynasties (1368-1911), stories and dramas mainly advocated good, denounced evil and propagated traditional morality through fantastic plots and vivid characters. This type of New Year Pictures has been favored for hundreds of years by the Chinese people.

Stories

It was created on the basis of folktales that were popular among the people, including historical tales, mythology, and folklore. The key elements in the composition lay in the plot outline.

Fish Swallowing Ink When the Ink-stone Is Washed (signifying success in the imperial civil examination): Wuqiang, Hebei

Meng Haoran Riding a Donkey in the Snow: Wuqiang, Hebei

Meng Haoran Riding a Donkey in the Snow

The great poet Meng Haoran (689-740), of the Tang Dynasty, is pictured riding a donkey in the snow in search of plum blossoms. It shows that the poet paid the greatest attention to natural scenery. His poems possessed a simple style with deep and clean conception, mostly describing the scenes of mountains and rivers and his reclusive life as a hermit.

Ma Gu Presenting a Birthday Gift to the Queen Mother of the Western Heavens

Ma Gu, a goddess of ancient mythology, would gift glossy ganoderma wine, which she had made on the banks of the Jiangzhu River, as a birthday present to the Queen Mother of the Western Heavens, on the 3rd day of each Lunar third month. Thus, people usually put up this New Year print to express their congratulations for elders' birthdays.

Ma Gu Presenting a Birthday Gift to the Queen Mother of the
Western Heavens: Wuqiang, Hebei

Qilin Delivering a Baby: Jinnan

Chang'e Flying to the Moon:
Yangliuqing, Tianjin

Yellow River Battle Formation

This was adapted according to one episode in Chinese mythology in *Canonization of the Gods*. During the reign of King Yinzhou of the Shang Dynasty (c.IIth century BC), three sprites, Yunxiao, Bixiao and Qiongxiao from Sanxian Island, created this "Yellow River Battle Formation" along the Yellow River, to avenge their brother Zhao Gongming. After hearing of the situation, Supreme Master Lao Zi descended to the world to help people break the Yellow River Battle Formation and kill the three sprites.

Yellow River Battle Formation: Fengxiang, Shaanxi

The Mouse Marries off a Daughter

This was adapted from a popular folk story. It is a satire about a mouse's daughter wanting to marry a rich and powerful husband. She had already been refused by the sun, the cloud, the wind and a wall. In the end she married her natural enemy – the cat. Themes involving mice were popular among people, with its allusions to life and propagation because of the strong procreative abilities of mice.

The Mouse Marries off a Daughter: Mianzhu, Sichuan

Three Monkeys Tricking a Pig in a Game of Chinese Dominoes

This sketch was created at the end of the Qing Dynasty (1644-1911) and the beginning of the Republic of China (1912-1949) with a view of criticizing society. Three tricky monkeys and one fat pig are pictured sitting around a square table playing *paijiu* – Chinese dominoes. The three tricky monkeys are cheating by exchanging cards under the table using their feet, unbeknownst to the fat pig, busy dallying with a beautiful woman. The image of the fat pig alluded to those rich people wallowing in fleshpots. The general appearance of this New Year Picture was lively, with delightful and humorous sentiment. What was more, it lashed out at social evils through entertainment.

Three Monkeys Tricking a Pig in a Game of Chinese Dominoes: Mianzhu, Sichuan

Stories and Dramas

Coin-bearing Tree

It shows an episode in the Sichuan opera, *Coin-bearing Tree*.
Zhang Sijie, a fairy maid of the Jade Emperor, descended to the
world and married a poor scholar named Cui Wenrui. Seeing the
poverty of the Cui family, Zhang Sijie gathered her fairy sisters to
build pavilions in the garden and planted a coin-bearing tree. It
was said that gold coins blossomed on the tree and would re-grow
after being shaken off.

Coin-bearing Tree: Mianzhu, Sichuan

Dog Barking at the "God of Fortune"

Dog Barking at the "God of Fortune": Mianzhu, Sichuan

In the past, the custom of worshipping the God of Fortune was popular in the western regions of Sichuan. Some beggars would dress themselves up as "Military Fortune Gods" and distribute images of the God of Fortune to each family. In this way, they would also sing auspicious ditties and beg for money from people. In this picture, a greedy "Military Fortune God" does not seem satisfied with the charity provided, so the dog barks at him.

White Elephant Mountain

A plot, taken from the Chinese classic *Strange Tales from the Liaozhai Studio*, tells us that a poor scholar named An Youyu lost his way while trying to pass through Mount Hua. He accidentally lodged himself with a family of roe who had disguised themselves as human beings, and he fell in love with Huaguzi, the daughter of the family. The young scholar fell seriously ill due to his unbounded attachment to his lover after he left the family.

After she heard about it, Huaguzi hurried to find him and cure his illness. When An Youyu recovered, they were married. Later on, Huaguzi's father forced his daughter to return home, but the young scholar pursued the family over many days and nights. He was unfortunately poisoned to death by a snake demon. Huaguzi, however, rescued him by reviving him, telling him who she really was. In the end, they killed the snake demon together and led a happy life ever after.

White Elephant Mountain: Mianzhu, Sichuan

Dramas

This type of New Year Pictures emerged during the mid-Qing Dynasty (1644-1911). It mainly manifested the fantastic plotlines found in local operas, emphasizing the description of characters, and bestowing a particular lasting appeal to traditional dramas.

Heroes of the Yang Family

General Yang Jiye, a great hero of resistance against Khitan invaders, had seven sons who were valiant and skillful in battle. Unfortunately, most of his seven sons sacrificed their lives in battles for the country. In the end, his wife Madam She, when she was over one hundred years old, took up the post of marshal to lead the heroines of the Yang family to defend their borders and kill their enemies. In fact, the story of the *Heroes of the Yang Family* gained universal praise among the people.

Battle at Renyizhai: Fengxiang, Shaanxi

Heroes of the Yang Family: Weifang, Shandong

The Longevity Peach Feast

This depicts a scene from the Longevity Peach Feast given by the Queen Mother of the Western Heavens, with the immortals offering birthday greetings to her. The Queen Mother of the Western Heavens was a goddess responsible for longevity in Chinese mythology. The longevity peaches growing in her garden blossomed every 3,000 years, and bore fruit only after another 3,000 years. When the peaches of longevity ripened, the Queen Mother of the Western Heavens would invite immortals to attend a grand birthday feast on Lake Jasper. In this way, *Longevity Peach Feast* pictures were favored among the people for celebrating birthdays.

Longevity Peach Feast: Weifang, Shandong

White Pearl Pass: Weifang, Shandong

Scorpion Hole (from *Journey to the West*):
Fengxiang, Shaanxi

Exiled Life of Prince Chong Er

During the Spring and Autumn Period (770-453 BC), Prince Chong Er, the son of King Hui of the State of Jin, went into exile in the state of Chu (740-223 BC). One day, he came upon a huge swamp named Yunmeng, while hunting with the king of Chu, and encountered an exotic beast resembling a bear with a trunk, the head of a lion, tiger claws, jackal hair and an oxtail. It was much bigger than a horse, with black spots covering its body. The king asked Chong Er what on earth it was. One of Chong Er's escorts, Zhao Shuai, answered: "It is called a tapir, and can eat copper coins and digest them into water." Another escort named Wei Chou said he could catch it alive. Then, with the help of Zhao Shuai, he captured the tapir alive and gave it to the king of Chu as a gift.

The Son's Sacrifice for His Mother at Thunder Peak Pagoda

This scene is excerpted from the traditional opera *The Legend of the White Snake*, which tells us that a snake spirit named Bai Suzhen was imprisoned under the Thunder Peak Pagoda by a powerful monk named Fahai. Then 18 years later, her son Xu Shilin won first place in the imperial civil examination and came to visit her. His filial behavior moved the god of the pagoda, and he helped the son meet his mother at last. This picture contains allusions of commending honor, glory, loyalty and fealty among the people.

Save the Prince and Resolve Palace Intrigue

At the beginning of the Wanli Period (1573-1620) of the Ming Dynasty (1638-1644), Empress Dowager Li attended to court affairs behind a screen, because the emperor was too young to rule the state. She invited her father Li Liang to help her, but he instead conspired to usurp the throne. The Guardian Duke Xu Yanzhao and Vice-Minister of Ministry of War Yang Bo both came to the palace to pressure Empress Li to dismiss Li Liang, but the Empress refused to accede. Later on, Li Liang occupied Zhaoyang Palace and plotted the murder of both the crown prince and the empress. The Empress Li luckily awoke to what was really happening, and invited Xu Yanzhao and Yang Bo to enter the palace to prevent the coup and save the crown prince. In the end, she had her son ascend the throne, in her arms.

Li Cunxiao Lifting a Tiger:
Zhuxianzhen, Henan

Exiled Life of Prince Chong Er:
Zhuxianzhen, Henan

The Son's Sacrifice for His Mother at Thunder
Peak Pagoda: Zhuxianzhen, Henan

*Saving the Prince and Resolving Palace
Intrigue*: Zhuxianzhen, Henan

A Pair of Gold Talons

This retells a story of the reunion of two brothers, Ma Chao and Ma Dai. During the period of the Three Kingdoms (AD 229-263), their father, general Ma Teng, was executed because of his failure to assassinate Cao Cao. The two brothers raised troops to avenge their father, but were unfortunately defeated, and then suffered a long separation. Later, they had to confront each other in battle but did not recognize each other until they matched a pair of gold talons handed down from their ancestors.

A Pair of Gold Talons:
Zhuxianzhen, Henan

Pala Temple:
Zhuxianzhen, Henan

Pala Temple

This is extracted from the late Qing-dynasty novel *Shi Gong An* (*Cases Judged by Shi Shilun*). A local landlord named Fei Degong was attracted by a pretty girl as he traveled through the Pala Temple Fair, and wanted to force her to marry him. The girl preferred to die rather than marry him, and was beaten to death by the landlord. Huang Tianba reported the whole case to the righteous officer Shi Shilun. Chu Biao then set up a stratagem to successfully trap Fei Degong. Chu Biao and Zhang Guilan, the wife of Huan Tianba, pretended to be a father and daughter out on a stroll around the temple fair. Zhang Guilan had herself taken away by Fei Degong and then lured him to drink too much at his home. At midnight, she helped others enter and capture Fei Degong. This picture shows a scene of discussion about stratagems to catch Fei Degong.

Arresting the Satyr "Orchid"

This is also taken from the late-Qing novel *Shi Gong An* (*Cases Judged by Shi Shilun*). According to a report from the Magistrate of Leling County, dozens of thefts and sexual assaults had all been committed by a satyr known as "Orchid." He had always entered and left without a trace. Furthermore, he always drew an orchid on the wall after committing a crime. The county magistrate Shi Shilun sent his officers to secretly investigate, and they found the satyr sheltering in the Dragon King Temple. They then successfully captured the satyr at midnight. This picture shows the capture scene of the satyr "Orchid."

Arresting the Satyr "Orchid":
Zhuxianzhen, Henan

Butterfly Cup,
Zhuxianzhen: Henan

Butterfly Cup

Lu Shikuan, the son of Governor Lu Lin of Hunan and Hubei provinces, beat the fisherman Hu Yan to death because the old man had refused to sell him a giant salamander, despite his threats. Tian Yuchuan, the son of the Magistrate of Jiangxia County, could not tolerate this brutal behavior and killed Lu Shikuan. Tian Yuchuan was then sought by Lu Lin, and was fortunately saved by the fisherman's daughter, Hu Fenglian. They became engaged, and Tian Yuchuan gifted a butterfly cup, handed down from his ancestors, as a love keepsake to his young lady. Later on, Lu Lin led his troops to fight against Japanese pirates and enlisted Tian Yuchuan as a soldier. Tian Yuchuan rendered meritorious service and saved Lu's life in battle, so the governor married his daughter Lu Fengying to him. After the war ended, Hu Fengying appealed to the law court, with the butterfly cup as a proof. After a judgment from up high, Hu Fenglian became Tian Yuchuan's wife and Lu Fengying his concubine. This picture shows a scene of revelry in the bridal chamber on the wedding night of Tian Yuchuan and Lu Fengying.

Su San on the Way to Her Retrial under Escort

The courtesan Su San fell in love with Wang Jinlong and refused to receive clientele any longer. The procuress wanted to sell her to the rich merchant Shen Yanlin as his concubine for profit. Shen's wife slept with another man and poisoned Shen to death. She falsely accused Su San of killing her husband in the local court. The county magistrate took bribes from Shen's wife and sentenced Su San to death. Chong Gaodao, who escorted Su San to Taiyuan for retrial, accepted her as his adopted daughter after he heard of her sufferings.

Su San on the Way to Her Retrial under Escort: Liangping, Sichuan

Beating His Princess Wife (paper-cuts for window
decoration): Wuqiang, Hebei

Beating His Princess Wife

All ministers and generals accompanied by their children went
to pay homage to Guo Ziyi, a great general of the Tang Dynasty
(618-907), on his eightieth birthday. However, Princess Shengping,
the daughter of the Emperor Su, did not wish to offer her
congratulations with her husband, Guo Ai, the son of the General
Guo Ziyi. So, her husband, the emperor's son-in-law, scolded and
beat her for her disgraceful insolence. This picture was divided into
four sections. The first was that of Guo Ai beating the princess
in a rage, and the princess returning to the palace to cry out her
grievance; the second, of General Guo Ziyi binding his son and
sending him to the court to apologize; the third, of the emperor
and empress comforting the princess; and the fourth, of her being
consoled by the Emperor Suzong and Empress, and after a sincere
apology from Guo Ai, the young couple reconciling again.

Lü Bu Flirting with Diao Chan

This is also known as *Series of Stratagems*. At the beginning of the 3rd century, the military tycoon Dong Zhuo monopolized power with the assistance of his adopted son Lü Bu, threatening the Han court with upheaval. The Prime Minister Wang Yun wanted to neutralize them and save the court. One of his female entertainers named Diao Chan offered him a series of stratagems to sow discord and kill Dong Zhuo and Lü Bu. In the end, Dong Zhuo was killed by his adopted son Lü Bu. The picture shows Diao Chan acting in a charming manner in Lü Bu's arms while casting innocent eyes on Dong Zhuo, who in a fury raises his spear to stab Lü Bu.

Lü Bu Flirting with Diao Chan (Xiangdishu New Year print):
Caoxian County, Shandong

Yao Gang Conquering the South

Yao Gang, the son of Yao Qi, a famous general of the Han Dynasty (202-220 BC), accidentally beat to death Guo Rong, the father-in-law of the emperor, and the Emperor Liu Xiu decided to have him executed. When General Yao Qi learned of this, he captured his son and sent him to the court to apologize. Most of the military generals begged the emperor to spare Yao Gang's life. Finally, the emperor withdrew the death penalty but exiled him to the south. When Yao Gang passed Hubei on his way to exile, he had to confront a malicious local landlord named Huang Gang, and ultimately killed his whole family to uphold justice. The scene shows Yao Gang fighting against Huang Gang's cunning wife.

Yao Gang Conquering the South (Xiangdishu New Year print):
Caoxian County, Shandong

The Monkey King Wreaking Havoc in the Heavenly Palace
(Xiangdishu New Year print): Caoxian County, Shandong

图书在版编目（CIP）数据

民间年画：英文 / 蓝先琳编著．

—北京：外文出版社，2008

（中国民间文化遗产）

ISBN 978-7-119-04675-4

Ⅰ．民… Ⅱ．蓝… Ⅲ．年画—简介—中国—英文　Ⅳ.J218.3

中国版本图书馆 CIP 数据核字（2008）第 092711 号

出版策划：李振国

英文翻译：曲　磊

英文审定：May Yee　　王明杰

责任编辑：杨春燕

文案编辑：刘芳念

装帧设计：黎　红

印刷监制：韩少乙

本书由中国轻工业出版社授权出版

民间年画

蓝先琳　编著

© 2008 外文出版社

出版发行：

外文出版社出版（中国北京百万庄大街 24 号）

邮政编码：100037

网　　址：www.flp.com.cn

电　　话：008610-68320579（总编室）

　　　　　008610-68995852（发行部）

　　　　　008610-68327750（版权部）

制　　版：

北京维诺传媒文化有限公司

印　　刷：

北京外文印刷厂

开　本：787mm×1092mm　1/16　印张：10.25

2008 年第 1 版第 1 次印刷

（英）

ISBN 978-7-119-04675-4

09800（平）

85-E-647 P